Girl into Fox

6/19/19

For Jenny,
thanks for being
such a great
inspiration!

Chrisma

Girl into Fox

Poems by

Christine Hamm

ISBN: 978-1-949229-87-5

Kelsay Books
Aldrich Press
www.kelsaybooks.com

To the Chan Family, without whom these poems would not exist

Contents

"Their redness talks to my wound, it corresponds.
They are subtle: they seem to float, though they weigh me down,"
Tulips, by Sylvia Plath

The September After

I still
remember when

you lay
under me and closed
your eyes

your face so full
of blood and

distance the gold
dust and paper wings:

ignoring that same question

Visitor's Lounge

in this room
I feel
I deserve to die

not die
exactly just
fade/fall to shreds

like a bright
blue umbrella

I am
telling myself

stories about a wolf

in winter breaking
the snow's crust

as I slip my
fingers down to

your throat

A Thousand Islands

The sun slipped
into the burnt

hills' envelope
at four. I wrote

his name in
the crook

of my elbow,
remembering

how you and I
fought at the corner,

how
I threw your car
keys away

and walked
alone
to the post office.

I rose, lost
in a street light.
The boy with the missing

tooth said he liked

the hollow spot
in my side.

A blue Toyota
drove by slowly
with the windows down.

A gull landed
on a nearby
spruce—its call
a church bell.

Directions for a Morning Ritual

Remember that blue

is not your friend. Dream of the gray
horse, Mitzy, who bit a camper's

leg right after you got the little
girl to trust you. Pretend you are

a small black spaniel. Chase a red
ball and swallow it. Swallow a string.

Use a feather
in a such way that it is destroyed

by rain. Draw a picture of a sandbox.
Each grain of sand with

its own shadow. Argue with your dead
daughter about the color of the sky, your hand.

Double Happiness

looks like two eights.
A snow plow drags
continously
past molting Christmas trees,

yellow shuttered
noodle shops.

By the ice-glazed parking lot,
salt-stained cars slip
into Ninth Avenue
and gash each other.

How did confetti and
thistles grow
such jagged houses?

Sea gulls swipe at the knotted
red plastic bags clotting the sidewalk,
flexing their frozen claws
like someone
readying himself
for a punch.

The boy next door
stumbles out
into the cardboard
yard in his underwear

and I bang
on the window
to ask him
what's happening to me.

Under torn prayer flags,
wind chimes bang
like a lamb's feed pail.

Notes from the Wolf's Den

mothers like crowned skeletons
receiving radio transmissions
from four decades ago

at a party of plastic rubies and crystal
laughter from under the bed

crinolines helped them float
across the weather like a river

whispering charm bracelets
taught them when

conditions are optimal
fingers burn like candles
and flesh tastes like soap

Back Stroke

In a pink stadium-
sized hall filled

with vomiting
children, I learned

to breathe.

Never
allowing pool
water

above the crown
of my head.

There in the milky
shallows, I floated

in the arms
of someone

else's mother.

Burnt Fields

I don't watch the mirror. I am in love
      with the weeping girl downstairs.
In my dreams, the light fades with a violet undertone,
         a half-heard song.

My childhood was the size of a closet,
      an unlit red room stinking of earth,
dead animals and hunger, while the record player rasped
         a polka in the front yard.

Me and My Heart Try to Bury the Body

In the cemetery I feel sleepy
I am tired of kissing

so I climb the fence
but keep falling down

people kill chickens at the gates
to appease a different god

than the one you always imagined
yourself to be—

Samantha Before the Fire

A raven plays his piano
on the front lawn; robins supervise
while boys in ragged

hoodies kick the ball
across the street and back—girls
in masks and feathers

are cowboys and Indians.
You shoot me and I die. You lay me
on the front steps, my spine

crooked, awkward, and circle
me with dandelions and daisy-chains.
You kneel and study

my face, biting your lip,
clasping your hands. I watch through
my eyelashes. Your mother

approaches, smearing
the dim yard with blasts of headlight.
The sun leaves slowly, leaking

orange—turning the sky
yellowish white. Somewhere inside, your
dog barks. Footsteps on gravel.

My back twinges and the boys
yell, their hands hitting rubber with the sound
of desperate insects at a window.

The Arsonist's Biography

This door opens to your crawlspace,
to hoarded piles of burnt hair & hotel matches.

Your mother whispers, *don't freak out,* as she adds
a teaspoon of pink gasoline to the pancake batter

& flings last year's stuffed animals under
the kerosene truck in your front yard.

This door opens to your bedroom, where the horse
sleeping in your bed dreams it's an invisible girl

& as the girl slips down a chimney,
the horse shivers, feeling its throat burn.

Ode to an Eye

Purple and white trumpet flowers
with the same violent center. Spiders

and butterflies dangle and clasp. Sun-
flowers so head-heavy they lean and fall.

Perfect round morning glories with a dark
five-point-star stamped in each. Some

climbing vines are yellowing, drying
to husks. The starling and cow bird

look almost identical to me. A cat chirps
behind me on the porch. Now the trumpets are pink,

not purple, as sparrows and a plane dip
through the faint blue sky. All brown and

gray clay, a mourning dove watches me from
the stunted flowering tree. I cannot name half

these plants. The prayer flags I hung last year
have faded, shredded—this, too, gives me

comfort. The trunk of the fig tree has surreal bends—
its leaves like infant hands grasping and releasing.

How to Jonah

The sky is an orange face. The sky is tan without really meaning it.
Bury your notions in the whale. The whale in the middle of mall,
the mall under the library. You forgot you were at the beach, selling
hotdogs and hats. A mongoose snakes into your lap. Stroke its ears
and tell it about the girl. There's a ton of dirty gears under your
feet. Whisper to your pets, *I have a god in this fight.*

I Smell Animal, Like an Animal

as he sits on my toes

the wolf's eyes are yellow and round

like the egg of a particularly cruel bird

right now the sky is shaped like an apology

the one I owe my brother for his car

if he could ever pick up the phone

from his crystal nest underground

Some Are Horses

polish and horse tears smear my hands
my boots yanked in the tack room
my hair sticks to snaffle bits and
swaying dressage bridles

my pinto waits, his eyes
follow my hands, ears flick bob,
as I fling saddle over stall door

my face thrusts into his neck
I breathe slow, tongue tip on fur

he shifts from hoof to hoof
stomps at a fly

I make a cradle of my hands
and he rests his chin there
velvet, trembling

Notes from the Underground Palace

I grew to love the Japanese beetles
devouring my apple

tree now just a stick a jut of brown
pointing up like

an accusing tongue "no sweets" says
the bumper sticker

on the battered red Toyota fake
snow bundled next

to the garbage someone is trying
to make it winter again

a dragonfly flies into your mouth
and stays there

Your Boat

You call for me as if I could hear, your voice
   a phone's drowsy ring.

(I feel most myself when I am falling)

After you knot cords around a cleat, you tuck
   my sky-blue baseball cap under the photo

of my mother kneeling,
under the cracked bowl of porridge.

(ashes, ashes, we all fall down)

You shuck your bloody deck shoes over the gunnel.

I left your names for me: *mousetrap,*
rat bait, poison cake.

The clouds vomit
like a sick daughter.

Blueprint for the Reenactment

The field died elsewhere, was
transported here after. The cows

and elm branches have been
coached. Holly bushes have

been added for atmosphere,
and the sky puffed full of pink

and yellow clouds. An angry
girl in a red dress is standing

in for the sun, who refused
to cooperate. The bedraggled

poodle is me, and you, the violent
mist, the broken place in the

fence with the black nails
pointed just so.

Aftermath

Later, the moon drops
down over the wrecked

cars, white and wheezing.
Humidity coils around

bent steering-wheels,
pummeled engines,

the torn seats of Datsun
hatchbacks and sedans.

When I said, *I'm sorry
I hurt you,* I was lying.

The Wrong One

I have been forgetting how evil I am,
by filling the furniture up with lies.
I am trying to soften myself.
I shave my armpits on Wednesday.
I split my tongue on the weekend.
You are the wrong one to tell this to.
I ask my dead pets for forgiveness,
but they are on vacation
in the public lake.

The public lake asks
for a thousand dollars,
in order that it may be fed safely,
and I remember I collected safety
glass in my blue box
with the bent dancer—
Thinking it was diamonds.

Landscape with Burning Bridges

I am not a poet,
says a lamb.
This is not
a poem, says a wolf.

This is where
the dreams
belong,

where they surface,
bedraggled,
dust covered,
coughing,

pawing at their delicate

noses. Lace
of wolves' breath:
My dad has taken

my brother by the throat,

and is banging
the back of his head
against the garage.

Screams in the trees.

My mother curls
into a ball
under the kitchen

table. This god,
golden and bare-chested,
becomes bigger

or smaller depending
on how

I hold him in my palm.

On Witches, III

my violet felt cloche tipped
over one ear, my mouth a red
bow the size of a city block

your feelings pour from my throat
in the shape of a girl's first knife

you told me, *you're dead,*
you don't need to worry about

whether the color of your eyes
matches lace or boot soles

the radio says, *come down with me,*
and we smear ourselves with glitter

and the boiled fat
of our kindergarten teachers.

For the Angel of Abandon

I drove a Pinto over a cliff without waking up.
I drove a Porsche into a light pole without hearing the music stop.

You were there with me
both times, small, trying not to die.

I burned my hand in the kitchen fire, the scar
like a dragon's mouth.

At night, the animals ravaging the garden sang my name,
the noise an unpleasant sigh.

And my mother said, *always let him win.*

Repetition Compulsion

My head full
of cotton, wool.

My head
full of dulled
needles, cracked

spoons.

He was a fawn
missing his back
hoof, something chewed

off, pasty.

When I was all
alone in that love.

Yellow, ratty—

a hair color
I could never achieve.

A baby to hold,
a worm
that wriggles and
wriggles

but never quite falls—

The Alchemical Reunion

Plastic red tablecloths, mosquitoes, potato salad, stifled laughter.

I write on my palm,
     "You invited God into the house/and burned the house
down".

I hum, *are you my mother?* until my voice goes gray.

          Is this my home you're showing me, or is this another
trick?
               1. Refinish the kitchen floor of bone and buttons.
               2. Hang the bunting with lace and teeth marks.

I can only taste ash, someone's daughter said,
the meatloaf in front of her.

Ramona the Fallen

Crooked, rectangular eyes.
The stench of the horses

we knit ourselves to. Her ears
clotted with gold/diamond circles

she tugged until her scabs opened
their mouths. Hurling down her

shining silver pony, she broke
the fence with her collar-bone—

the poles banging together
with a sound like wooden bells.

Faint stars where she went into
herself with an exacto knife, a stapler:
I break everything to make it fit.

After the Accident

seatbelts hanging us upside down
can't feel my right wrist

still a little stoned on teenaged sex
and the fight about the cupholder

a branch nods through the windowshield,
the car ticking like a wind-up toy slowing down

                             shattered dome light in my hair,
          I unfasten and fall to the ceiling

crimson and clover/over and over/crimson and
                                 still on the radio

(you crawl as if you had lost something small)

a slow volcano bump begins on my forehead

leaves fluttering down from the tree
we crushed

voices outside
        a shouting like children in sprinklers.

Like Hand-Grenade Daughters

In the dawn
garden, the wolves
drift

from our bare legs.
You say, *Mom*
always kissed you

better.

We wrestle
in the flowerbeds,
soil clogging

our ears.
Like stars
we burn

what's left: gristle,

fingernails, bruised heels—

These pills,
oh,
these white fallen
apples.

Cinders

The angel of the electric fence, how my brother
and me put it in our mouths.

Whispering, sorry sorry sorry
to those wobbly spotted calves.

Pink hooves galloping and stumbling
to the broken edge. Haze of alfalfa

and dung clinging to my hair.
In the dank pool by the ditch:

algae clumps brush our shoulders
like an uncle's wet kiss.

Without Presence

The red-headed flies spin
above my hands.

They hover as I take
myself apart and spread

my parts into the garden.
Tomorrow like a god

I will rise whole again,
write "house bound"

upon your face.
The rotten pears

I have left
out in the sun

will be swarming with gods,
and the gods will

look like bees or that cat
your mother has stowed

in the freezer
since your last birthday.

My Minor God, My Silver Saint

five of us, maybe four

acolytes, apostates, groupies, topless
in hot pants because you were tacky

my mantra, as you could have guessed,
was *gun-shy*

bullet right to the third eye, where
you tied me with your mother's

scarves to the bed
so we could start again

now, there's no limit to how
many times I can come

or how boring you are
when you pretend to be human

Little Drummer Boy

Barefoot,
I climbed

telephone
poles, teetered

from the top.

Firemen came,
but not for me.

You liked
to experiment:
what burned best

on the electric coil.

The babysitter forgot
about the rice,
and then the eggs,

and then bed.

I ate
a pillow in my
dream and then

woke up
still hungry.

Brown Horse with a Paper Horn

A girl and a man twice her size comb
through a windblown field, their faces
sad, her skin a broken-out map.

You with the eggs taped under
your shirt, you with the collection
of sheet music and filthy fish tanks,

this is where I fall in love with you.
Nothing happens in the right order.
The lost girl is never found. The small

girl grows up small, surrounded by
animal-shaped mirrors. All good things
happen in reverse – we start to forget

to feed our former fish, grow tender for our
violin-enhanced future. The problem starts
when the girl disappears at the 7-11, or right
when her penguin scarf is found.

Dress Rehearsal

Someone calling, *Mira, Mira, not so close.*
A white lake. Something frozen, stepping
on something frozen and uneven. The seagulls
clatter, pull the clouds into filaments. The moon,
a lopsided mouth, enters your body and you
drown again. Last time I held you, your breath
like wet dishrags and worms. A house hidden
under a painted sheet. The fire doesn't help you.
In that tank top with the ducks across, holding
yourself, shivering, not looking at me. The lake
breaks up and away. Birches are falling around
your library: snow falls, but no one listens.
You hum as you stomp your naked feet. The fire
doesn't help. You say your house is burning,
I say mine is sinking, even now.

Your Boat

Sewing and fishing are the same:
patience, repetition, blood.

I am sewing a red bird to the hem of your
        work jeans, right where Mom's fingernails
                        tore off a chunk.
You sing "Lucy in the Sky
        is Crying," pinching the Angus yearlings
     in the steerage with a tuning fork, chortling.

Here in the library of empty waves, everyone
        is wishing you'd take off in your day-glo heliocopter.

The librarian waves for help with a flag
        made with what's left of her underwear.
You jump
onto my lap, chew your fingernails and twitch.
The librarian turns up the white
        noise, hoping you'll be drowned out.

She straightens her straw hat, coughs and growls,
        buries a bone with her little paws
in the copyrighted sky.

Huge white flakes sift down from the clouds, cover the stern,
the mast. A loose sail whips in the windless buzz,

you grab my ear with your greasy
        thumbs, whisper, *that part's*
          called the shroud.

The snow turns into slow, feeble moths,
     either drunk or dying. One lands on your eye. You call
for *more salt, more ketchup.*

We all fall past the waves, into the earth,
                    into the shoebox of your accident.

The water starts over with what's left.

The Green One Piece

You are trying to teach me to breathe
underwater. The pool is bright,

the same color as the underside
of my tongue. The women sunning

at the edges sing something I can't
understand. Your body is heavy and

cool: it shakes with laughter on top
of me. I watch the blue swirl

of paper clips and barrettes
around the pool drain; I remember

the mouse I found floating
like a wet sock last week—

its soft triangular head,
the fleshy lace of tiny fingers.

Accelerants

Cue the bruised
girl, laughing hysterically. Cue the seedy
mary jane, a bikini bottom

with elastic
unraveling, a slippery diving board.
Now the drunk man, with dim

references to paternity. Now
a tree swinging up to meet her face.
Now speeding tickets, his fight

with a policeman. Now a mother,
a brother, spreading and thinning like spilt
water into the dusk-colored rooms.

Heat Lightning

Clumps of bees hover and land;
wolves pick through the garbage

dump next door. She watches
from a stool under a feeble oak

in the backyard, making holiday
cards for sale on the weekend,

one folding table at the flea market.
She sews the face of a little girl

on heavy watercolor card stock—
three black stitches for the hair,

pink knots for the cheeks, wearing
gloves so the sweat of her hands

won't stain the paper. The paper is
faint blue, the sky just as the sun

is starting to rise. Her sky is dim,
churning like milk spilled into a

glass of water. The wolves swoon
in the heat, fall to their sides to pant

on broken mattresses. She wipes
tears from her chin with her wrist,

swears softly to herself. Without wind, the oak leaves rattle.

A Cat will Show its Wide Mouth as Way of Saying Hello

When I was first able to walk, I fell into a doll. I named her (—-) until my grandmother hit that name out of my mouth. We wore identical cotton frocks: red with black camellias, a black ribbon tied at the neck. Lace at every opening, stiff, ugly as bark. I fed her tinsel along with the yellow cat. With the screen door open, the animals started to come inside. I named her Christine because I couldn't imagine another word. I stared at the pink wall next to my bed with my hands over my ears. The wall receded. The pink became liquid. Everyone's face wore a frown that day, and someone was put in the fireplace. My father laughed and laughed when a women's hair caught fire. But that was another party.

I Try to Say Beautiful Without Using the Word

In this song, it sounds like "button" or "sky." The tulips in the dollar store are too bright to cause much pain. Poly-ester and wire—it makes for interesting breakfast. I weave the fake flowers into your hair, pretend you will wake up. So many things are buried in that backyard. I found a doll foot once, solid, cement-like, stained. The tiny toes were not even painted. Pennies and pennies. Plastic barrettes, faded to sky-color. The snow is up to my knees now. My breath freezes inside my mouth, mini icicles I swallow and swallow. I said "mini" when I meant "many." What have you learned since then? Why do verses repeat: to make the song long enough. Real pearl buttons, down every girls' blue sweater.

New Year

I. **unending**
in and out, phoenix-like, zombie-like
in the x-files, scully once got a tattoo of a snake on her ass
the ouroboros, which means a snake eating its tail
it can be drawn using different methods
and often wears a dragon's head

II. **the most effective gun is in the hands of child**
I try to write 1 slash 2 as a date, but it keeps auto-
correcting to one half

I dream that spiders go in at the mouth, so I use
toothpaste, then mouthwash, then Drano

When I say "you" I am often talking to my dead horse

I tell my husband I want a gravestone in titanium,
because that is the strongest metal I know

you suck at my elbow scabs, then eat them
you like the texture of my yellow hair, so you eat that too,
although it hurts when you yank it free

this is useless, he can't even read

Just a Cigar

Smoke stains the ceilings.
Above the stove, in the bathroom.
The walls in the dining room, the bedroom.
The windows are smeared, clotted with it.
Thumbprints whiten the doorknobs, the edges

of the refrigerator. The bedposts, the lock
on the bathroom door.
In the living room, the yellow
and orange bouquets on wallpaper
have darkened into wincing faces, into
kindergarten shapes,
right above what was his La-Z-Boy.

Metamorphosis

My hair burns white in the sun
as my father mixes sulfuric acid

on the asphalt driveway
to see what will melt.

The cats circle, my mother sings and cries
at a window. It rains and stops.

We sit in the mud. Chunks of the driveway
flake off, fall down the hill into the creek.

The house is tilting west. A doe comes
to the backyard, holding one front leg at a right angle.

Sometimes, the bark of an oak tree will
turn into a sleeping cat. The tree house

is filled with wasps and echoing screams.
He painted it orange and blue just for me.

Flour, powdered sugar. Water.
This is how I make dinner for the family.

Girl into Fox

I had a title
before a name—

"baby girl" and a black
footprint the size

of a man's thumb
on a folded

piece of paper.
I hated the girl who

stuttered and slipped
like me, hated her vapid

tears as she watched
the clouds fall.

They called her "never-was,"
not a sister or book,

so much more
loved than me. Today

I sit on my haunches
under the birdfeeder,

licking my elbow
while the doves eat

and groan. Even now,
your fingers are losing their power.

Notes on Remorse

that woe coated my brother
like filthy vaseline

and when he knocked
I pretended to be a tree house—
he was so thirsty, always

that he learned how
to light matches with the bottom
of his foot:

a house collapsing in a fog of ash.

that I couldn't touch
the six-year-old crossing the

street against the light,
his yellow baseball

cap winking like
an untethered astronaut.

Who are You and Why are You Following?

One of us is connected
to the other by a wet
string. One of us

is burying some-
thing in the sand.
Why am I holding

your hand, hoping you
will love me?
The sky is filled

with tilted mirrors,
the beach littered
with sighing mothers.

You gave me my
first velvet dress, and
told me I was stupid.

Someone's whispering
as I try to sleep
under the lake.

Can you hear it?
It's not a pleasant voice,
or the radio. Something angry
and feathered, a crow caught in string.

Ode to Love, part 12

The sun slides
up from the water

and the water
changes from black

to grey. Clouds gather
in the corner, pile on,

bleed violet and pink.
The moon fades so

quickly we find its
name hard to remember.

Snow and
sand are the same

from this distance.
I can't recall your voice

any more, or the words
you used to call me.

I answered
like a black dog,
a sleeping thing.

Thoughts on Seashells

If the world is upside down, then I am okay, watching the black dots inside my cats' ears gather, coalesce, move apart. If I were a good mother, he would have clean ears, all the mites flushed away. I am not a good mother, or a mother at all. All my children are either dead or imaginary. I was a daughter, once. It didn't take. She kept saying, "I can't wait until you are old enough and have to take care of me". I've never been old enough to be more than a disappointment. My parents and I are on two different paths. My path ends at the beach. Theirs ends at an empty tennis court. Both of us dying, on different sides of the country. I take care where I put my feet, but I am still constantly falling. The water is cold and bitter. I am not my mother, but I am cold. My cat says, *What does that even mean?* I bury myself in the sand, hoping that someday you will come and dig me up.

Electro Shock

Count backwards from nine hundred. *An ink flood with sharp stars slicing as they slip by.* Is the light too bright? *The stars bleed.* There now, we have moved it away. *Organs the color and shape of cauliflower.* The gown opens in the front. *Organs color the ceiling.* Please remove everything from the waist down. *A hum like slow wind chimes.* You may keep your toes on and your hair. Please show me where it began. Are you always this hairy? Zippers at the wrists and back of your hide so you can slip out. *Where again, where.* Latches at the back of your eyeballs, so they may be entered by God. Are you *A musical hum like slowed down radio. A series of numbers and decimals.* Please tell me where it started. *Red squares loosely tied to black squares. A heavy vibration.* Lie still. Are you always this? *Two wolves, silver and brown, tugging on pink meat between them.* A series of decimals, remember.

The Farm Vacation

The slow tick of the electric fence,
the smell of baked dirt and tires. Animals:

absent-eyed, everywhere—dusty,
neglected, gaunt. Pigs, cats, trembling

dogs and chickens. All hooves splitting,
unshod. The saddles wormy and cracked.

Every horse I rode bled from the mouth. Still,
I dug my spurs in, drove them to jump

the bales I hauled and stacked in the paddock:
I was working on my form. What is a horse,

if not transport? On the ground, my riding
boots tipped and struggled. What is a girl,

if not a rack of unprocessed meat? When
I wasn't riding, I lay in the corn fields to escape

my cousins. Something in my mouth kept me
from sounding fully human. I thought only

about winning and hiding
that summer, before I learned to drive.

Ten Pounds

You are not a dog sleeping;
you are a girl. You dream

you are eating the rump
of a piglet while a circle

of lions pick at mints stuck
between their toes. You are

trying to save the pig. You
are trying to vomit the flesh

you already ate. High above
is a window painted with

circles and stars, too tiny
for your hand to open.

The gold hair cluttering the frame
drifts, catches on your lips.

Notes on Warming

Two polar bears stroll across the wall,
one poised and thoughtful, the other

watching me, a little hungry, a little sad.
The microwave beeps every few minutes—

something has been left inside for a long
time. Outside the window, it is hot and

raining—the air smells like gas and asphalt.
A chair has tipped over in the kitchen.

I don't remember it. We spoke last night,
all the lights off, we spoke so late—

now the light hurts and the front
door is open, still unlocked.

The Absence of Shame

Black snakes on the white curtains
almost too small to make out.

The carpet in my bedroom had
been a light green, radiant, before

the dogs got to it. The transparent
dress my mother made me wear

to the supermarket, how she
called me, *easy to make.* My bed

collapsing, such an old thing,
with the noise of a car crash

or waterfall. Each wall of the room
was papered with my feelings—

my mother saying, that day
we spent in the woods picking

pinecones to spray gold, *why don't you
draw some roses for a change?*

Landscape with Veiled Observer

A deer is picking her
way slowly through

the snow, a front leg tucked
to her chest.

Chickadees, cardinals scold
and sway in the stunted pines—

somewhere, a wind chime
is clanging.

A handful of flung pigeons
circle the sky.

Under the frozen
birdbath, a small fox

waits, her fur spiked like crystals,
mostly buried.

Acknowledgments

The author would like thank Kelsay Books for all their help with this manuscript, and Karen Kelsay specifically for selecting my book for publication.

In addition, the author would like to thank the following publications for publishing poems in this collection: *Dime Show Review, Posit, pioneertown, New Welsh Review, Tinderbox Poetry, American Chordata, Ditch Poetry, Rufous City Review, The Pinch, Kenning Journal,* and Erbacce Press, UK, for publishing an earlier version of some of these poems in the chapbook, *My Western.*

About the Author

Christine Hamm lives and teaches in New Jersey. She has a PhD in English and is getting her MFA at Columbia. She recently edited an anthology of creative works inspired by Sylvia Plath (called *Like a Fat Gold Watch*) and has been published in *Denver Quarterly, Nat Brut, Rhino, Painted Bride Quarterly* and many others. Blaxevox published her third book, *Echo Park*, and, in 2018, Ghostbird Press published her sixth chapbook, *Notes on Wolves and Ruin.*